# Devotional Poems

# to

# Strengthen, Encourage

# and

# Inspire

Illustrations by
Daquita & Batinna Mosley

# Table of Contents

Acknowledgments

I would like to acknowledge first and utmost God, who is the head of my life. By His inspiration, I have written these poems. He is "My Confidant" bringing me through "The Valley". I would like to acknowledge my mom and dad, who encourage me and are always there for me. I would like to acknowledge my children, siblings, friends and co-workers for their support of faith in making my desire for this publication become a reality.

## Dedications

I dedicate "The Healing Man" to Batinna Mosley, my youngest daughter, who goes to God for healing of her body when she is feeling sick. To Robin Ware and Paula Anderson who have experienced God's miraculous healing power in their lives.

I dedicate "Death" to my mother-in-law for the death of her second son. Perceita Beasley for the death of her daughter. April Cook-Lopshire for the death of her first husband, Pastor David Cook. These women are learning that even when God takes someone very dear to our heart, it is for a reason even though we may not understand.

I dedicate "Humble yourself" to Brenda Holloway, as she asks God for continued strength in this area of her life.

I dedicate "My Confidant" to Daquita Mosley, my oldest daughter, who is learning that God is her confidant and that she can go to Him for everything; Ronnie E. Ware, Jr., who is seeking Him in his life, may he never stop. To pre-teens, teenagers, and adults seeking a true friend.

Dear Reader,

I pray as you read each poem and passage of scripture, they will help strengthen, encourage, and inspire you as you seek a closer relationship with God. These poems were inspired by God and written by me. Each poem is my personal testimony of my walk with God on what I have been taught through His grace.

My first poem, Protective Wings, was inspired on April 16, 1998. I was at work in downtown Nashville when God inspired me to write that poem. I was unaware of tornado warnings out that day. I started my morning off meditating on the Lord, as I do every morning, with no distraction of television or radio. As I traveled to work that morning, I was curious as to why vehicles were pulled over to the shoulder of the road. Still unaware of the tornado warnings, I continued my drive to work. After getting to work a co-worker informed me of the tornado warnings out that morning.

Shortly after I wrote Protective Wings, the tornado was ten minutes away from downtown and vastly approaching our area. All of my co-workers evacuated the office except Mr. Randy Phillips and me. As I sat at my desk with God's perfect peace that no harm would come to me, Mr. Phillips convinced me to go downstairs with the others. By the time we got downstairs the tornado struck in a matter of seconds. Our building received no damage while others received minimal damage. God had his Protective Wings over our building that day.

Within six weeks time, He inspired me to write the poems that are written in this book. I pray they strengthen, encourage, and inspire you as you continue to walk in His grace.

Sincerely,

Geneva Mosley,
WinnerForGod

# Devotional Poems

# to

# Strengthen, Encourage

# and

# Inspire

## *PROTECTIVE WINGS*

I have protective wings over me.
Wings the human eye cannot see.

Words can't express this joy I feel.
Because I know that God is real.

I have to endure many, many tests.
I will not stop; my feet will not rest.

It's hard for people to understand.
Because their eyes cannot see this man.

This man who's there through thick and thin.
This man who knows that "I CAN."

I can do all things through Christ
which strengtheneth me.
All things the human eye cannot see.

This man who fights my battles for me.
This man the human eye cannot see.

This man who makes a way out of no way.
This man who lightens up my day.

A light that shines brightly over me.
A light the human eye cannot see.

Wings that calm my every fear.
Wings that wipe away my tears.

I have protective wings over me.
Wings the human eye cannot see.

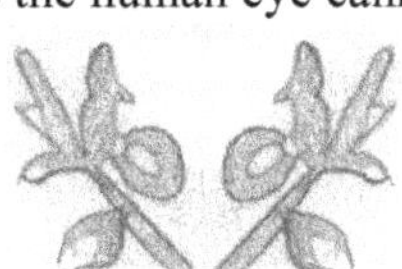

*I can do all things through Christ, which strengtheneth me.*

Ph 4:13

*Ye are the light of the world. A city that is set on a hill cannot be hid.*

*Let your light so shine before man, that they may see your good works, and glorify your Father which is in heaven.*

Mt 5:14,16

*The Lord shall cause their enemies that rise up against thee to be smitten before thy face: they shall come out against thee one* way, *and flee before thee seven ways.*

Dt 28:7

*Peter therefore was kept in prison: but prayer was made without ceasing of the church unto God for him.*

*And when Herod would have brought him forth, the same night Peter was sleeping between two soldiers, bound with two* chains: *and the keepers before the door kept the prison.*

*And, behold, the angel of the Lord came upon him, and a light shined in the prison: and he smote Peter on the side, and raised him up, saying, Arise up quickly. And his chains fell off his hands.*

Ac 12:5-7

*And that we may be delivered from unreasonable and wicked men: for all* men *have not faith.*

*But the Lord is faithful, who shall stablish you, and keep you from evil.*

II Thes 3:2-3

ꕥ
✧
ꕥ

## *GOD IS REAL*

God is real, He lives today.
Yes God is real and showing me the way.

The way and path that leads to Him.
He opened His door I entered in.

Real in my heart, real in my soul.
Real in my life, He made me whole.

To be made whole is so divine.
He made me whole just in time.

In time to receive His wondrous grace.
In time before I leave this place.

This place called Earth, where sin resides.
To a better place, my Savior's side.

I'm Heaven bound, I won't turn back.
I'm Heaven bound, I'm on the right track.

The track that leads to eternity.
God is real and lives in me.

God is real, He lives today.
Take heed and listen to what I say.

*"Blessed Assurance"*

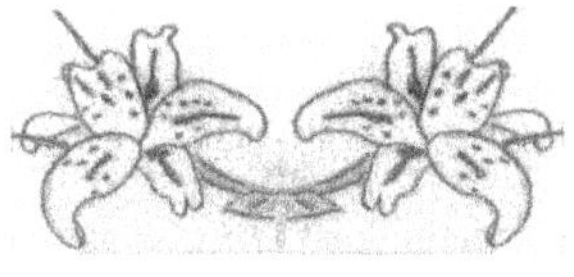

❄
✞
❄

*But this I confess unto thee that after the way which they call heresy, so worship I the God of my fathers, believing all things which are written in the law and in the prophets.*

Ac 24:14

*To him give all the prophets witness, that through his name whosoever believeth in him shall receive remission of sins.*

Ac 10:43

*But to him that worketh not, but believeth on him that justifieth the ungodly, his faith is counted for righteousness.*

Rm 4:5

*That if thou shalt confess with thy mouth the Lord Jesus, and shalt believe in thine heart that God hath raised him from the dead, thou shalt be saved.*

*For with the heart man believeth unto righteousness; and with the mouth confession is made unto salvation.*

*For the scripture saith, Whosoever believeth on him shall* not *be ashamed.*

Rm 10:9-11

## *COMMITMENT*

I' m making a Commitment to Thee
Oh Lord,
To live according to your word.

I make a Commitment to you today,
And won't go back on what I say.

I give my life Lord unto thee,
Change my life Lord set me free.

Help me Lord be your child,
Help me as I cross each mile.

Each mile dear Lord I cross and do,
Brings me closer Lord to you.

I made a Commitment I won' t turn back,
Help me Lord go down the right track.

Help me Lord I will not rest,
Help me Lord pass each test.

The tests and challenges you have for me,
On Faith, Patience, and Love for Thee.

I know dear Lord it will be hard,
Protect me, keep me, be my guard.

Guard me Lord against sin and shame,
Until I see your face again.

I made a Commitment to Thee dear Lord,
To live according to your word.

*"Amazing Grace"*

ஐ
✧
ஐ

*Then said Jesus unto his disciples, If any man will come after me, let him deny himself, and take up his cross, and follow me.*

*For whosoever will save his life shall lose it: and whosoever will lose his life for my sake shall find it.*

*For what is a man profited, if he shall gain the world, and lose his own soul? Or what shall a man give in exchang for his soul?*

*For the Son of man shall come in the glory of his Father with his angels; and then he shall reward every man according to his works.*

*Verily I say unto you, There be some standing here, which shall not taste of death, till they see the Son of man coming in his kingdom.*

Mt 16:24-28

*Blessed is every one that feareth the Lord; that walketh in hisways.*

*For thou shalt eat the labour of thine hands: happy shalt thou be, and it shall be well with thee.*

Ps 128:1-2

*But now, after ye have known God, or rather are known of God, how turn ye again to the weak and beggarly elements, whereunto ye desire again to be in bondage.*

Gal 4:9

*When thou vowest a vow unto God, defer not to pay it; for* he hath *no pleasure in fools: pay that which thou hast vowed.*

*Better is it that thou shouldest not vow, than that thou shouldestvow and not pay.*

Ec 5:4-5

❄

## *A BABE*

A babe is how I come to you.
You said it's something we must do.

You said we must be born again,
Without this you can't enter in.

Enter in Lord and help me grow.
Feed my mind and feed my soul.

Your word is proper nourishment.
It's what I need to give me strength.

I'll eat dear Lord what you have to give.
I'll eat dear Lord so I may live.

For you no matter what may be.
Live for you so others may see.

That if I live my life for you,
All the wonderful things you do.

I'm your child, I'll make you proud.
I'm your child, I'll sing it loud.

Loud enough the world will hear.
Just how much you really care.

You care for them, you care for me.
A babe is how I came to be.

A babe is what I have to be,
To grow in you and live for Thee.

❖
🕊
❖

*Jesus answered and said unto* him, Verily, verily, I say unto *thee, Except a man be born again, he cannot see the kingdom of God.*

Jn 3:3

*In that hour Jesus rejoiced in spirit, and said, I thank thee, O Father, Lord of heaven and earth, that thou hast hid these things from the wise and prudent, and has revealed them unto babes: even so, Father for so it seemed good in thy sight.*

Lk 10:21

*WHEREFORE laying aside all malice, and all guile, and hypocrisies, and envies, and all evil speakings,*

*As newborn babes, desire the sincere milk of the word, that ye may grow thereby:*

I Pt 2:1-2

*For when for the time ye ought to be teachers, ye have need that one teach you again which be the first principles of the oracles of God; and are become such as have need of milk, and not of strong meat.*

*For every one that useth milk is unskilful in the word of righteousness: for he is a babe.*

Heb 5:12-13

*But ye are not in the flesh, but in the Spirit, if so be that the Spirit of God dwell in you. Now if any man have not the Spirit of Christ, he is none of his.*

*For as many as are led by the Spirit of God, they are the sons of God.*

Rm 8:9,14

ജ
✧
ജ

## *SACRIFICE*

A sacrifice was made for me.
God gave His son on Calvary.

The blood stained cross is the price He paid.
That very day a promise was made.

To save this world from hate and sin.
To grant us love and peace within.

What would I have to sacrifice,
In order for God to enter my life?

No price too much, no price too big.
I must repay Him for what He did.

I'm in debt to you Lord, I owe you my life.
I'm in debt to you, for you paid the price.

I'm here dear Lord, I bow to you.
I'm here dear Lord, what shall I do?

To please you Lord in my life.
I'm willing Lord to sacrifice.

Things of this world can't go with me.
Tell me Lord what shall it be?

God sacrificed His son for me,
And I will give my life to Thee.

❄
✞
❄

*For God so loved the world, that he gave his only begotten Son, that whosoever believeth in him should not perish, but have everlasting life.*

Jn 3:16

*Fear not little flock; it is your Father's good pleasure to give you the kingdom.*

*Sell that yee have, and give alms; provide yourselves bags which wax not old, a treasure in the heavens that falleth not, where no thief approacheth, neither mothe corrupteth.*

*For where your treasure is, there will your heart be also.*

Lk 12:32-34

*And when he was gone forth into the way, there came one running, and kneeled to him, and asked him, Good Master, what shall I do that I may inherit eternal life?*

*Then Jesus beholding him loved him, and said unto him, one thing thou lackest: go thy way, sell whatsoever thou hast, and give to the poor, and thou shalt have treasure in heaven: and come, take up the cross, and follow me.*

*And he was sad at the saying, and went away grieved: for he had great possessions.*

Mk 10:17,21-22

***THE HEALING MAN***

I know a man with the power to heal.
Regardless how bad you may feel.

He hears your sorrows and your woes.
He feels your pain from head to toe.

He heals your body, mind, and soul.
He has the power and this I know.

I know because this man healed me.
I went to Him and gave Him my plea.

Father, I come before you now.
Heal my body for you know how.

Heal my body cause I believe.
I' ll stand firm and wait to receive.

What you have prescribed for me.
Stand on my FAITH and trust in Thee.

My FAITH in Thee will prevail.
My FAITH in Thee will never fail.

Your office is open all day long.
Your prognosis is never wrong.

Your prescribed medication is FAITH
in you.
To trust in all the things you do.

I gave it to you Lord and I believed.
I took my medication and you healed me.

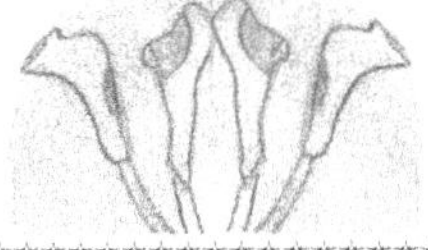

ꕥ
✧
ꕥ

*And his fame went throughout all Syria: and they brought unto him all sick people that were taken with divers diseases and torments, and those which were possessed with devils, and those which were lunatick, and those that had the palsy; and he healed them.*

Mt 4:24

*And Jesus went about all the cities and villages, teaching in their synagogues, and preaching the gospel of the kingdom, and healing every sickness and every disease among the people.*

Mt 9:35

*And a woman having an issue of blood twelve years, which had spent all her living upon physicians, neither could be healed of any,*

*Came behind him, and touched the border of his garment: and immediately her issue of blood stanched.*

Lk 8:43-44

❄
✞
❄

***FAITH***

Faith is the substance of things hoped for,
the evidence of things not seen.
God is FAITH, He's my life, and
my everything.

Have FAITH in Him and no one else,
and soon you will see.
That FAITH in Him and no one else,
will open doors for thee.

Have FAITH in Him and no one else,
He is always near.
Have FAITH in Him and no one else,
there's no need to fear.

Have FAITH in Him and no one else,
He never lets you down.
Have FAITH in Him and no one else,
He'll turn your life around.

Have FAITH in Him and no one else,
it's worth the sacrifice.
Have FAITH in Him and no one else,
His son has paid the price.

If we have faith in our life,
sin will not abide.
Because He's there to protect,
and to be our guide.

*Now faith is the substance of things hoped for, the evidence of things not seen.*

*But without faith it is impossible to please him: for he that cometh to God must believe that he is, and that he is a rewarder of them that diligently seek him.*

Heb 11:1,6

*That Christ may dwell in your heart by faith, that ye, being rooted and grounded in love,*

*May be able to comprehend with all saints what is the breadth, and length, and depth, and height;*

Eph 3:17-18

*THEREFORE being justified by faith, we have peace with God through our Lord Jesus Christ;*

*By whom also we have access by faith into this grace wherein we stand, and rejoice in hope of the glory of God.*

Rm 5:1-2

*For as the body without the spirit is dead, so faith without works is dead also.*

Js 2:26

## *PATIENCE*

Grant me patience Lord today.
Grant me patience on my way.

Help me see and understand.
I need patience in this land.

With all the people in my life.
Husband, children, or my wife.

I need patience Lord in Thee.
Grant me patience, hear my plea.

With strangers as they cross my path.
Patience Lord is what I ask.

In my daily walk with you.
In all the things I try to do.

Patience Lord I ask of Thee.
Grant me patience, hear my plea.

*I returned, and saw under the sun, that the race is not to the swift, nor the battle to the strong, neither yet bread to the wise, nor yet riches to men of understanding, nor yet favour to men of skill; but time and chance happeneth to them all.*

Ecc 9:11

*Better is the end of a thing than the beginning thereof: and the patient in spirit is better than the proud in spirit.*

*Be not hasty in thy spirit to be angry: for anger resteth in the bosom of fools.*

Ecc 7:8-9

*For when God made promise to Abraham, because he could swear by no greater, he swear by himself,*

*Saying, Surely blessing I will bless thee, and multiplying I will multiply thee.*

*And so, after he had patiently endured, he obtained the promise.*

Heb 6:13-15

*My brethren, count it all joy when ye fall into divers temptations;*

*Knowing this, that the trying of your faith worketh patience.*

*But let patience have her perfect work, that ye may be perfect and entire, wanting nothing.*

Js 1:2-4

## *OBEDIENCE*

Obedient Father I need to be.
Obedient Lord unto thee.

Unto your word and way to go.
Show me Father I don't know.

Tell me Father things to do.
To live a life that pleases you.

Tell me Father show me the way.
How I need to walk each day.

Teach me Father I'm your child.
To be obedient, meek, and mild.

To love each other as you love me.
Show me Father help me see.

Ways of the world, ways of sin.
What I must do to enter in.

The Gates of Gold way up high.
There in Heaven by your side.

Show me Lord what I must do.
To be obedient unto you.

*But this thing commanded I them, saying, Obey my voice, and I will be your God, and ye shall be my people: and walk ye in all the ways that I have commanded you, that it may be well unto you.*

Jer 7:23

*Then Peter and the other apostles answered and said, We ought to obey God rather than man.*

*The God of our fathers raised up Jesus, whom ye slew and hanged on a tree.*

*Him hath God exalted with his right hand to be a Prince and a Saviour, for to give repentance to Israel, and forgiveness of sins.*

Ac 5:29-31

*And why call ye me, Lord, Lord, and do not the things which I* say?

Lk 6:46

❄
✞
❄

## *THE VALLEY*

The valley is deep; the valley is wide.
Lord help me reach the other side.

This journey's long I may get weak.
I need you Lord to guide my feet.

I need you Lord; I need you now.
I need you Lord to show me how.

Show me Lord, show me today.
Show me Lord this I pray.

I pray dear Lord for strength in thee.
I pray dear Lord please help me see.

My way through the wind and rain.
Comfort me Lord, ease my pain.

Dry the tears from my weeping eyes.
Help me Lord so I might rise.

Above this valley here below.
Please guide me Lord as I go.

I will not doubt; I will be strong.
If I trust in thee I can't go wrong.

Until I get there, the other side.
Please dwell in me Lord, please reside.

*"Precious Lord"*

❖

❖

*I will lift up mine eyes unto the hills, from whence cometh my help.*

*My help cometh from the Lord, which made heaven and earth.*

*He will not suffer thy foot to be moved: he that keepeth thee will not slumber.*

*Behold, he that keepeth Israel shall neither slumber nor sleep.*

*The Lord is thy keeper: the Lord is thy shade upon thy right hand.*

*The sun shall not smite thee by day, nor the moon by night.*

*The Lord shall preserve thee from all evil: he shall preserve thy soul.*

*The Lord shall preserve thy going out and thy coming in from this time forth, and even for evermore.*

Ps 121

## *I NEED YOU*

I need you Lord to guide my feet.
To make me humble, mild, and meek.

I need you Lord prepare my path.
To do the things that you ask.

I need you Lord, I need your light.
To guide me in the dark of night.

I need Faith Lord to believe.
What I can do and receive.

Promises you made to me.
I need you Lord please help me see.

Wisdom and guidance till the end.
That keeps me from the life of sin.

I need you Lord this I pray.
I need you Lord I' ll never stray.

From the way of your word.
Keep me please I ask dear Lord.

Keep me Lord so I may see.
That it' s in you I need to be.

It' s you dear Lord that I need.
Hear my cry Lord, hear my plea.

❄
✞
❄

*HEAR my prayer, O Lord, give ear to my supplications: in thy faithfulness answer me, and in thy righteousness.*

*And enter not into judgement with thy servant: for in thy sight shall no man living be justified.*

*For the enemy hath persecuted my soul; he hath smitten my life down to the ground; he hath made me dwell in darkness, as those that have been long dead.*

*Therefore is my spirit overwhelmed within me; my heart within me is desolate.*

*I stretch forth my hands unto thee: my soul thirsteth after thee, as a thirsty land. Selah.*

*Hear me speedily, O Lord: my spirit faileth: hide not thy face from me, lest I be like unto them that go down into the pit.*

*Cause me to hear thy lovingkindness in the morning; for in thee doI trust: cause me to know the way wherein I should walk; for I lift up my soul unto thee.*

*Deliver me, O Lord, from mine enemies: I flee unto thee to hide me.*

*Teach me to do thy will; for thou art my God: thy spirit is good;lead me into the land of uprightness.*

*Quicken me, O Lord, for thy name's sake: for thy righteousness' sake bring my soul out of trouble.*

*And of thy mercy cut off mine enemies, and destroy all them that afflict my soul: for I am thy servant.*

Ps 143

*Cast thy burden upon the Lord and he shall sustain thee: he shall never suffer the righteous to be moved.*

Ps 55:22

❖

❖

## *HUMBLE YOURSELF*

Humble yourself before the Lord.
Heed to what is in His word.

Humble yourself put down your pride.
He wants a chance to dwell inside.

Humble yourself to receive.
Humble yourself and believe.

Things that He can do for you.
Believe in what He says is true.

Heed to what He has to say.
Don't let pride get in the way.

We must be humble, meek, and mild.
And come to Him just like a child.

To learn the wonders He can do.
The wonders that reside in you.

Pride can steal and rob you blind.
Pride will get you left behind.

When God comes back to earth again.
To take what's His away from sin.

To the place He said will be,
Life with Him eternally.

Humble yourself, put pride away.
Humble yourself in Him today.

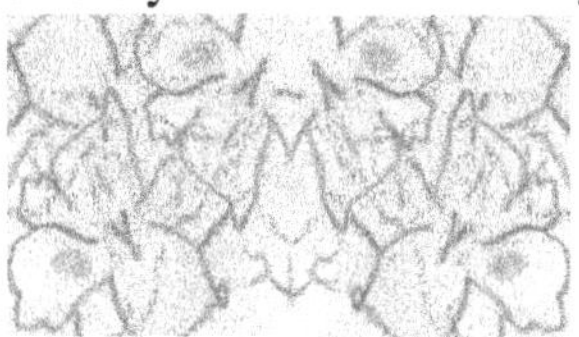

*Whosoever therefore shall humble himself as this little child, the same is greatest in the kingdom of heaven.*

Mt 18:4

*LORD, my heart is not haughty, nor my eyes lofty: neither do I exercise myself in great matters, or in things too high for me.*

*Surely I have behaved and quieted myself, as a child that is weaned of his mother: my soul is even as a weaned child.*

*Let Israel hope in the Lord from henceforth and for ever.*

Ps 131

*But he giveth more grace. Wherefore he saith, God resisteth the proud, but giveth grace unto the humble.*

Js 4:6

❄
✞
❄

## *MY SHEPHERD*

You're my Shepherd I'll follow you,
Show me Lord what I must do.

Give me direction guide my path,
To do the things that you ask.

If at times I go astray,
I need you Lord to show the way.

I need my Shepherd by my side,
To light my path and be my guide.

Your word is food for me to eat,
To make me strong when I feel weak.

And if I thirst you're there for me,
With songs of praise to give to thee.

Give me shelter from the rain,
Heal my heart when I feel pain.

There's no place I'd rather be,
Then in the special care of thee.

Be my Shepherd Lord today,
I need direction on my way.

I want to be part of your flock,
I need you Lord to be my rock.

Protect me from the Wolf called sin,
Give me joy and peace within.

*Behold, I send you forth as sheep in the midst of wolves; be ye therefore wise as serpents, and harmless as doves.*

Mt 10:16

*VERILY, verily, I say unto you, He that entereth not by thy door into the sheepfold, but climbeth up someother way, the same is a thief and a robber.*

*But he that entereth in by the door is the shepherd of the sheep.*

*To him the porter openeth; and the sheep hear his voice; and he calleth his own sheep by name, and leadeth them out.*

*And when he putteth forth his own sheep, he goeth before them, and the sheep follow him: for they know his voice.*

*And a stranger will they not follow, but will flee from him: For they know not the voice of strangers.*

*I am the good shepherd and know my sheep, and am known of mine.*

*As the Father knoweth me, even so know I the Father: and I lay down my life for the sheep.*

Jn 10:1-5,14,15

*For ye were as sheep going astray; but are now returned unto the Shepherd and Bishop of your souls.*

I Pt 2:25

ꕥ
✦
ꕥ

## *MY CONFIDANT*

Lord, you are my Confidant and my dearest friend.
I' ll confide and trust in you until the very end.

I share with you my hopes and dreams
and secrets of my heart.
Because of you, I' ve been redeemed
and have a brand new start.

A brand new start on my life is what
you' ve given me.
Myself, my mind, and my soul is what I
give to Thee.

I'll live for you, I won' t look back
there' s nothing left to see.
You saved me from my sinful ways
and gave me liberty.

If I fall or make mistakes you keep
them to yourself.
You pick me up, forgive me, I hold
your hand for help.

Your hand is strong, your hand is firm
and shows me what to do.
I' ll stand strong, I won' t do wrong and
only live for you.

I thank you Lord for being there and
lending me your ear.
For Lord you are my Confidant and I
know you care.

*"I must tell Jesus"*

❄
✞
❄

*He found him in a desert land, and in the waste howling wilderness; he led him about, he instructed him, he kept him as the apple of his eye.*

Dt 32:10

*And the scripture was fulfilled which saith, Abraham Believed God, and it was imputed unto him for righteousness: and he was called the Friend of God.*

Js 2:23

*It is better to trust in the Lord than to put confidence in man.*

*It is better to trust in the Lord than to put confidence in princes.*

Ps 118:8-9

*Henceforth I call you not servants; for the servant knoweth not what his lord doeth: but I have called you friends; for all things that I have heard of my Father I have made known unto you.*

Jn 15:15

## *WORDS*

Some Words were said to me today,
That put my heart Lord in dismay.

These Words Dear Lord I will forgive,
For I' m your child, in you I live.

Lord help me ease this pain I feel,
Lord help me as my heart is healed.

I' ll look unto your glorious light,
To ease my pain throughout the night.

For in you Lord is strength each day,
Help me see Lord guide my way.

To forgive and love this *man*,
And never look back on it again.

To show *him* love in all I say,
That love resides in you today.

Above in Heaven is love for *he*,
Above in Heaven is liberty.

Above in Heaven is peace within,
That keeps us far away from sin.

Help me forgive words people say,
That put my heart Lord in dismay.

*IN my distress I cried unto the Lord, and he heard me.*

*Deliver my soul, O Lord, from lying lips, and from a deceitful tongue.*

*What shall be given unto thee? Or what shall be done unto thee, thou false tongue?*

*Sharp arrows of the mighty, with coals of juniper.*

*Woe is me, that I sojourn in Mesech, that I dwell in the tents of Kedar!*

*My soul hath long dwelt with him that hateth peace.*

*I am for peace: but when I speak, they are for war.*

Ps 120

*Let no man deceive you with vain words: for because of these things cometh the wrath of God upon the children of disobedience.*

*Be not ye therefore partakers with them.*

Eph 5:6-7

*Wherefore, my beloved brethren, let every man be swift to hear, slow to speak, slow to wrath:*

*For the wrath of man worketh not the righteousness of God.*

Js 1:19-20

❄

## *FORGIVENESS*

Forgiveness is something we must do.
God forgives me and He forgives you.

He forgives us every day.
And helps us as we go our way.

We must forgive what people do.
And let God's love come shining through.

In your life, in Him today.
We must forgive, in this I pray.

Forgive your neighbor and your friend.
Let them see God dwells within.

Through your life they will see.
God is real and lives in thee.

Forgive your brother, forgive today.
Forgive your brother, this I pray.

Forgive your brother, he meant no wrong.
We must forgive, we must be strong.

Forgiveness is something we must do.
God forgives me and He forgives you.

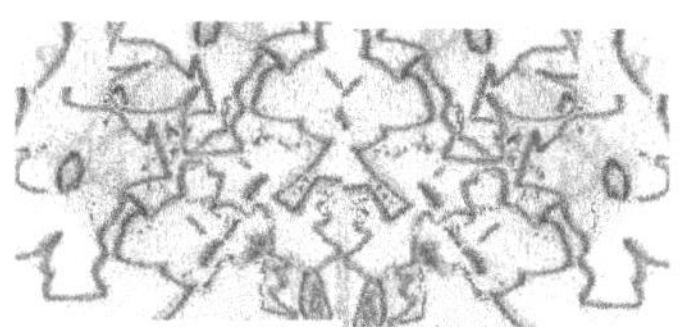

*For if ye forgive men their trespasses, your heavenly Father will also forgive you:*

*But if ye forgive not men their trespasses, neither will your Father forgive your trespasses.*

Mt 6:14-15

*Judge not, and ye shall not be judged: condemn not, and ye shall not be condemned: forgive, and ye shall be forgiven:*

Lk 6:37

*Take heed to yourselves: If thy brother trespass against thee, rebuke him; and if he repent, forgive him.*

Lk 17:3

ঌ
✦
ঌ

## *THE BLIND MAN*

A blind man is someone who cannot see.
I wonder who can this blind man be.

Blind to the Lord, His wonder, and grace.
So blind they can't see His smiling face.

Saying, if you come and live for Me.
I'll grant you life and set you free.

From the bondage and shackles of sin.
It's not hard just let Me in.

Your heart, your mind, and your soul.
Let Me have full control.

The blind man's critical and judgmental too.
With all the things He's done for you.

The joy and peace, words can't express.
God's in my life, I'm truly blessed.

With the eyes and power to see.
All the things He's done for me.

I opened my heart; He opened my eyes.
He made me meek, strong, and wise.

To the things I could not see.
Thank you Lord this isn't me.

A blind man is someone who cannot see.
I wonder who can this blind man be.

*For I tell you, that many prophets and kings have desired to see those things which ye see, and have not seen them; and to hear those things which ye hear, and have not heard them.*

Lk 10:23-24

*But their minds were blinded: for until this day remaineth the same veil untaken away in the reading of the old testament; which veil is done away in Christ.*

II Cor 3:14

*And beside this, giving all diligence, add to your faith virtue; and to virtue knowledge;*

*And to knowledge temperance; and to temperance patience; and to patience godliness;*

*And to godliness brotherly kindness; and to brotherly kindness charity.*

*For if these things be in you, and abound, they make you that ye shall neither be barren nor unfruitful in the knowledge of our Lord Jesus Christ.*

*But he that lacketh these things is blind, and cannot see afar off, and hath forgotten that he was purged from his old sins.*

II Pt 1:5-9

## *JUDGE*

To Judge your brother is wrong to do.
How you Judge him God judges you.

Don′t stand back and mock *his* life.
Instead encourage in times of strife.

Let *him* see God's love in you.
Let God's light come shining through.

Your walk in God, your walk in Thee.
Share with *him* and let *him* see.

The Joy and Peace that dwells within.
How Joy and Peace resides in Him.

Don′t Judge *his* life, don′t give *him* shame.
Life eternal is *his* to gain.

Say come my friend you will see.
Just how great our God can be.

He′s there for you through thick and thin.
He′s there for you please let Him in.

Yes, He′s our God, yours and mine.
He′s very loving and very kind.

To Judge your brother is wrong to do.
How you Judge *him* God judges you.

*JUDGE not, that ye be not judged.*

*For with what judgment ye judge, ye shall be judged: and with what measure ye mete, it shall be measured to you again.*

*And why beholdest thou the mote that is in thy brother's eye, but considerest not the beam that is in thine own eye?*

*Or how wilt thou say to thy brother, Let me pull out the mote out of thine eye; and, behold, a beam is in thine own eye?*

*Thou hypocrite, first cast out the beam out of thine own eye; and then shalt thou see clearly to cast out the mote out of thy brother's eye.*

Mt 7:1-5

*Speak not evil one of another, brethern. He that speaketh evil of his brother, and judgeth his brother, speaketh evil of the law, and judgeth the law: but if thou judge the law, thou art not a doer of the law, but a judge.*

*There is one lawgiver, who is able to save and to destroy: who art thou that judgest another?*

Js 4:11-12

*For all have sinned, and come short of the glory of God.*

Rm 3:23

❄
✞
❄

## *WISDOM*

Wisdom Lord I need in you.
Teach me Lord what I must do.

To receive blessings from Thee.
Give me direction, please show me.

The way in which my feet should go.
Show me Lord things I don't know.

Grant me Wisdom, give me light.
Show me Lord what is right.

In all the things I never knew.
Knowledge in what pleases you.

Wisdom Lord I ask today.
To resist temptation that comes my way.

Give me knowledge to understand.
I must please you and not please man.

I'll please you Lord and do what's right.
Guide me Lord throughout the night.

To places I thought could never be.
Through grace and wisdom please show me.

The way to go and live for you.
And give you praise in all I do.

*Wisdom strengtheneth the wise more than ten mighty men which are in the city.*

Ecc 7:19

*And even as they did not like to retain God in their knowledge, God gave them over to a reprobate mind, to do those things which are not convenient;*

*Being filled with all unrighteousness, fornication, wickedness, covetousness, maliciousness; full of envy, murder, debate, deceit, malignity; whisperers,*

*Backbiters, haters of God, despiteful, proud, boasters inventors of evil things, disobedient to parents,*

*Without understanding, covenant breakers, without natural affection, inplacable, unmerciful:*

*Who knowing the judgment of God, that they which commit such things are worthy of death, not only do the same, but have pleasure in them that do them.*

Rm 1:28-32

*For they being ignorant of God's righteousness, and going about to establish their own righteousness, have not submitted themselves unto the righteousness of God.*

Rm 10:3

*Happy is the man that findeth wisdom, and the man that getteth understanding.*

*For the merchandise of it is better than the merchandise of silver, and the gain thereof than fine gold.*

*She is more precious than rubies: and all the things thou canst desire are not to be compared unto her.*

Prov 3:13-15

ꕤ ✦ ꕤ

## *ACKNOWLEDGE*

Acknowledge God in everything.
So in your life He may reign.

Acknowledge Him when you don't know.
What to do or where to go.

Acknowledge Him and you will see,
He will open doors for thee.

Acknowledge Him. Give Him control.
Acknowledge Him and He will show.

All the things He ask of thee.
Acknowledge Him and you will see.

Pleasing Him will give you Joy.
Pleasing Him will fill the void.

In your life pulling you down.
He will turn it all around.

The sooner you start you will see.
Acknowledging Him is VICTORY.

In the battles of your life.
Turning darkness into light.

That will open up your eyes.
To follow Him and make you wise.

Down the path He has for you.
Acknowledge Him in all you do.

❄
✞
❄

*Trust in the Lord with all thine heart; and lean not unto thine own understanding.*

*In all thy ways acknowledge him, and he shall direct thy paths.*

*Be not wise in thine own eyes: fear the Lord, and depart from evil.*

*It shall be health to thy navel, and marrow to thy bones.*

*Honour the Lord with thy substance, and with the firstfruits of all thine increase:*

Pr 3:5-9

*Whosoever denieth the Son, the same hath not the Father: [but] he that acknowledgeth the Son hath the Father also.*

I Jn 2:23

❖

❖

## *JOY*

The Joy dear Lord you give to me.
Grants me peace that man can't see.

My cup is full and overflows.
With so much Joy the world should know.

How it feels to have peace in Thee.
How it feels to be set free.

Joy they cannot understand.
Joy not seen by the eye of *man*.

It lifts my spirit in the air.
And lets me know that you are here.

By my side Lord guiding my way.
I have this Joy in you today.

Joy that lifts me off my feet.
And makes me strong when I am weak.

It makes me want to shout and sing.
You are my life and everything.

I thank you Lord for Joy in thee.
I thank you Lord for blessing me.

With so much Joy words can't express,
That life in you is truly bliss.

*His lord said unto him, Well done, thou good and faithful servant: thou hast been faithful over a few things, I will make thee ruler over many things: enter thou into the joy of thy lord.*

Mt 25:21

*He that believeth on me, as the scripture hath said, out of his belly shall flow rivers of living water.*

Jn 7:38

*For the kingdom of God is not meat and drink; but righteousness, and peace, and joy in the Holy Ghost.*

Rm 14:17

*Thou wilt shew me the path of life: in thy presence is fulness of joy; at thy right hand* there are *pleasures for evermore.*

Ps 16:11

*For your shame ye shall have double; and for confusion they shall rejoice in their portion: therefore in their land they shall possess double: everlasting joy shall be unto them.*

Is 61:7

## *THANK YOU LORD*

Thank you Lord for saving me,
From the pit of hell I was doomed to be.

You saved me Lord in the nick of time,
From life of sin and life of crime.

You picked me up and turned me around,
I thank you Lord I thank you now.

I' ll thank you Lord each day I live,
I' ll thank you Lord for what you did.

The more I give thanks unto you,
The more I' m blessed in all I do.

I thank you Lord; I thank you today,
I thank you Lord for guiding my way.

From the path that led to sin,
And the darkness from within.

Within me Lord I could not see,
You entered my heart and set me free.

Thank you Lord for saving me,
From the pit of hell I was doomed to be.

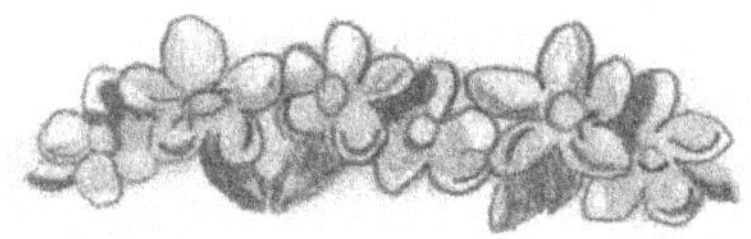

*O GIVE thanks unto the Lord for he is good: for his mercy endureth for ever.*

*O give thanks unto the God of gods: for his mercy endureth for ever.*

*O give thanks to the Lord of lords: for his mercy endureth for ever.*

*To him who alone doeth great wonders: for his mercy endureth for ever.*

*To him that by wisdom made the heavens: for his mercy endureth for ever.*

*To him that stretched out the earth above the waters: for his mercy endureth for ever.*

*To him that made great lights: for his mercy endureth forever.*

Ps 136:1-7

## *DEATH*

Death paid a visit to me today.
He took someone very dear away.

I' m not angry, just help me understand.
Why death paid a visit and took this *Man*.

This *Man* who' s been there by my side.
Who helped me, encouraged me, and was my guide.

Help me see it was your will.
Lord help me ease this pain I feel.

It hurts Dear Lord I cannot lie.
That this dear *Man* just had to die.

Lord give me strength to carry on.
I need you Lord, please make me strong.

Strong to make it through each day.
To yield to you in every way.

Thank you Lord for lending your ear.
Thank you Lord for I know you care.

You care for me cause I' m your child.
You care for me, please show me how.

To endure and look to you.
For wisdom and guidance on what to do.

Death paid a visit to me today.
He took someone very dear away.

❄
✞
❄

*Precious in the sight of the Lord is the death of his saints.*

Ps 116:15

*The righteous perisheth, and no man layeth it to heart: and merciful men are taken away, non considering that the righteous is taken away from the evil to come.*

*He shall enter into peace: they shall rest in their beds, each one walking in his uprightness.*

Is 57:1-2

*Be not deceived; God is not mocked: for whatsoever a man soweth, that shall he reap.*

*For he that soweth to his flesh shall of the flesh reap corruption; but he that soweth to the Spirit shall of the Spirit reap life everlasting.*

Gal 6:7-8

*But every man is tempted, when he is drawn away of his own lust, and enticed.*

*Then when lust hath conceived, it bringeth forth sin: and sin, when it is finished, bringeth forth death.*

Js 1:14-15

*A good name is better than precious ointment; and the day of death than the day of one's birth.*

*It is better to go to the house of mourning, than to go to the house of feasting: for that is the end of all men; and the living will lay it to his heart.*

*Sorrow is better than laughter: for by the sadness of the countenance the heart is made better.*

Ecc 7:1-3

## *HEAVEN*

Heaven is where I'm going to.
When my life on earth is through.

Until I get there I'll serve Thee.
Heaven's where I want to be.

I'll serve my Father until that day.
He takes His children far way.

To that place promised will be.
Life with Him eternally.

We must overcome this world below.
If Heaven's where we want to go.

It won't be easy, we must be strong.
And turn away from what is wrong.

If you don't know what to do.
Seek your Father, He'll show you.

The path to take, the way to go.
He's the only one that knows.

Which way to go and path to take.
The path that leads to Heaven's gate.

*"Goin' up Yonder"*

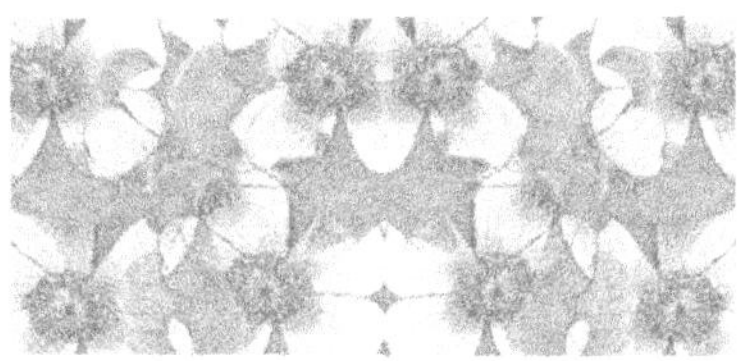

*Not every one that saith unto me, Lord, Lord shall enter into the kingdom of heaven; but he that doeth the will of my Father which is in heaven.*

*Many will say to me in that day, Lord, Lord, have we not prophesied in thy name? And in thy name have cast out devils? And in thy name done many wonderful works?*

*And then will I profess unto them, I never knew you: depart from me, ye that work iniquity.*

Mt 7:21-23

*AND I saw a new heaven and a new earth; for the first heaven and the first earth were passed away; and there was no more sea.*

*And I John saw the holy city, new Jerusalem, coming down from God out of heaven, prepared as a bride adorned for her husband.*

*And I heard a great voice out of heaven saying, Behold, the tabernacle of God is with men, and he will dwell with them, and they shall be his people, and God himself shall be with them, and be their God.*

*And God shall wipe away all tears from their eyes; and there shall be no more death, neither sorrow, nor crying, neither shall there be any more pain: for the former things are passed away.*

*And he that sat upon the throne said, Behold, I make all things new. And he said unto me, Write: for these words are true and faithful.*

Rev 21:1-5

❄

## *FISHERMAN*

God came one day and said to me,
A Fisherman is what you' ll be.

It takes no net, it takes no pole.
You' ll need *My* word and Faith to go.

Go and pass *My* word along.
*I' ll* give you help and make you strong.

It won' t be easy, it will be hard.
*I' ll* challenge you and take you far.

Far beyond the land and sea.
A Fisherman is what you' ll be.

*I' ll* give direction and guide your feet.
And lift you up when you feel weak.

*I' ll* give you water when the well is dry.
To feed the fish so they may try.

To live a life that pleases *Me*.
In their life *I* need to be.

A Fisherman is what I' ll be.
I' ll bring the fish Lord unto Thee.

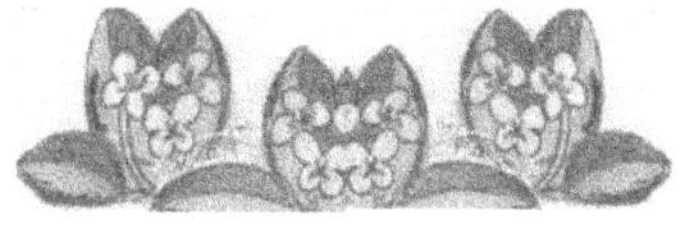

*And he saith unto them, Follow me, and I will make you fishers of men.*

*And they straightway left their nets, and followed him.*

Mt 4:19-20

*And a certain scribe came, and said unto him, Master, I will follow thee whithersoever thou goest.*

Mt 8:19

*For thankworthy, if a man for conscience toward God endure grief, suffering wrongfully.*

*For what glory is it, if, when ye be buffeted for your faults, ye shall take it patiently? but if, when ye do well, and suffer for it, ye take it patiently, this is acceptable with God.*

*For even hereunto were ye called: because Christ also suffered for us, leaving us an example, that ye should follow his steps:*

I Pt 2:19-21

### *GOD'S SMILE*

God sends His Smile to shine on me.
Through wind and rain or what may be.

His Smile gives warmth and peace within.
At times I'm down it makes me grin.

Grin and laugh the blues away.
He shined His Smile on me today.

His Smile help keeps my mind on Thee.
His Smile reminds me that I'm free.

The weight of this world I carry no more.
He closed and locked that sinful door.

He has the key and won't let go.
He has the key to my soul.

There's no place I'd rather be.
Then in His care under lock and key.

He stands secure by the door of my heart.
He stands secure and will never part.

God sends His Smile to everyone.
You must have eyes to see this SUN.

The SUN is more than eyes can see.
It's His Smile and it shines on me.

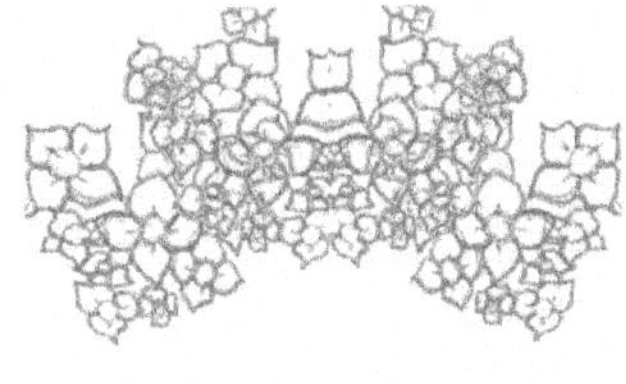

⁂

*Thank You*

⁂

www.ingramcontent.com/pod-product-compliance
Lightning Source LLC
Chambersburg PA
CBHW030949090426
42737CB00007B/549

* 9 7 8 0 9 7 7 8 0 0 3 0 8 *